FIND OUT ABOUT
WOOL & FIBRE

This edition 2002

© Franklin Watts 1994

Franklin Watts
96 Leonard Street
LONDON EC2A 4XD

Franklin Watts Australia
45-51 Huntley Street
Alexandria
NSW 2015

ISBN: 0 7496 4780 9

Dewey Decimal Classification 636.3

A CIP catalogue record for this book
is available from the British Library

Editor: Annabel Martin
Design: Thumb Design
Cover Design: Chloe Cheesman
Cover Knitting: Zoe Mellor
Picture Research: Alison Renwick

Additional photographs: Axminster
Carpets 10; J. Allan Cash Ltd 7, 26;
Bruce Coleman Ltd © Dr. Sandro
Prato 22 (both); Robert Harding
Picture Library © J.H.C. Wilson 19,
© Adam Woolfitt 29, © Tony Stone
Worldwide 16.

Printed in Hong Kong, China

FIND OUT ABOUT
WOOL & FIBRE

Henry Pluckrose

Photography by Chris Fairclough

FRANKLIN WATTS
LONDON•SYDNEY

This is a sheep.
It has a soft, woolly coat.
The coat is called a fleece.

Once every year the sheep is sheared.
The sheep-shearer uses electric clippers
to cut off its coat.
The fleece gives us wool.

We can also get wool from
the fleece of goats and llamas.
The angora is a breed of goat.
Its coat is as soft as silk.

The alpaca is a breed of llama.
It lives in South America.

After the fleece is cut off, it is cleaned and washed. The strands of wool are twisted together to make a long length of thread called "yarn." Long ago wool was spun by hand on a spindle . . .

or on a spinning wheel.

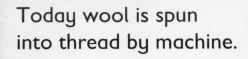
Today wool is spun
into thread by machine.

The spun wool is dyed to give it colour.

The coloured yarn is woven
into fabric.
A woven fabric is called a textile.
Fabric can be woven
on a hand loom
by a person called a weaver ...

but most of the textiles we use are woven in factories.

We wear clothes
made from woollen fabric.

Sweaters, gloves and socks
are knitted in wool . . .

and we use wool to make
curtains and carpets ...

rugs, cushion covers and many other things.

Not all textiles are made from wool.
The cotton plant grows
in hot, wet countries.
At harvest time
the seed pod bursts open.
The white fluffy fibre inside
is used to make cotton thread.

The cotton fibre is cleaned.
It is then spun, dyed
and woven into fabric.

Clothing made of cotton is light and comfortable to wear in hot weather.

Cotton is also used to make medical dressings.

We get silk from the silkworm.
A fully-grown silkworm spins
a silk case around its body.
These cocoons are collected
and the silk thread is unwound.

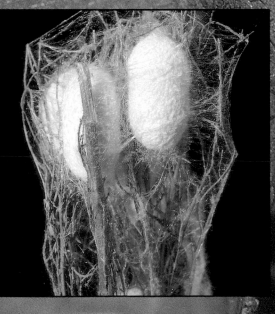

It is washed, spun and woven into fabric. Originally silk came from the Far East but it is now used worldwide.

Plants also give fibres
which can be spun and woven.
The stem of flax is soaked
in water, dried and crushed.
The fibres are then spun.

The fibres from flax
are used to make
a fine cloth called linen.
We use linen for sheets,
pillowcases, table-cloths
and kitchen towels.

This is the sisal plant.
The stem is broken
into tiny pieces
to give a fibre called sisal.

Sisal is used to make ropes.

The coconut palm is also used to give a tough fibre which can be woven.

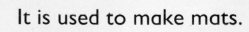

It is used to make mats.

Grasses, leaves and reeds give fibre.
This rattan basket is made
from the leaves of the palm tree.

100% COTTON ℗

MADE IN BRITAIN

	MACHINE MED. WASH	HAND
	WARM (60°C)	WARM (40°C)
	SPIN OR WRING	

The fibres mentioned in this book
are taken from plants and animals.
They are natural.
Other fibres are made in factories
using chemicals.
Look at the labels in your clothes.
Are you wearing something
made from cotton?
Or something made from wool?

MADE IN THE UNITED KINGDOM
PURE NEW WOOL
REINE SCHURWOLLE
PURE LAINE VIERGE
PURA LANA VERGINE
ZUIVER SCHEERWOL
REN NY ULD
HAND WASH WITH CARE OR DRY CLEAN ℗

About this book

This book is designed for use in the home, kindergarten and infant school.

Parents can share the book with young children. Its aim is to bring into focus some of the elements of life and living which are all too often taken for granted. To develop fully, all young children need to have their understanding of the world deepened and the language they use to express their ideas extended. This book, and others in the series, takes the everyday things of the child's world and explores them, harnessing curiosity and wonder in a purposeful way.

For those working with young children each book is designed to be used both as a picture book, which explores ideas and concepts, and as a starting point to talk and exploration. The pictures have been selected because they are of interest in themselves and also because they include elements which will promote enquiry. Talk can lead to displays of items and pictures collected by children and teacher. Pictures and collages can be made by the children themselves.

Everything in our environment is of interest to the growing child. The purpose of these books is to extend and develop that interest.

Henry Pluckrose